This book belongs to:

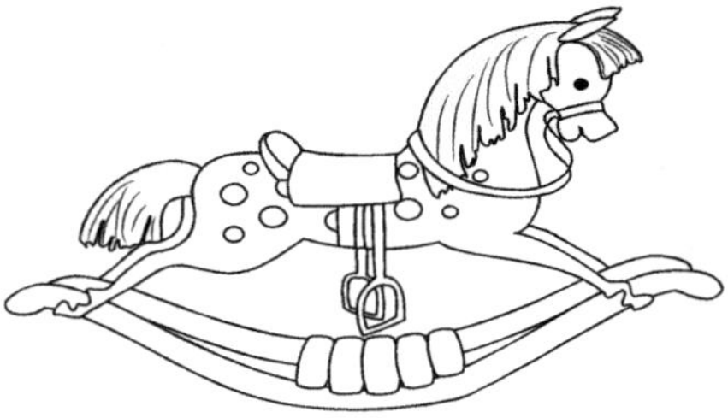

To A Very Sweet Goddaughter! Merry Christmas Coloring Card

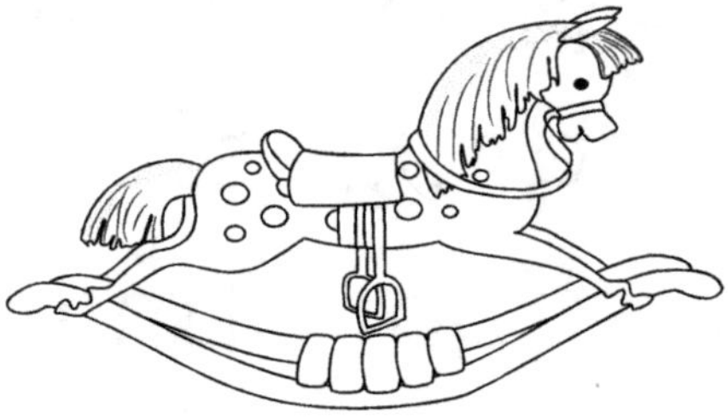

Joy to the world!

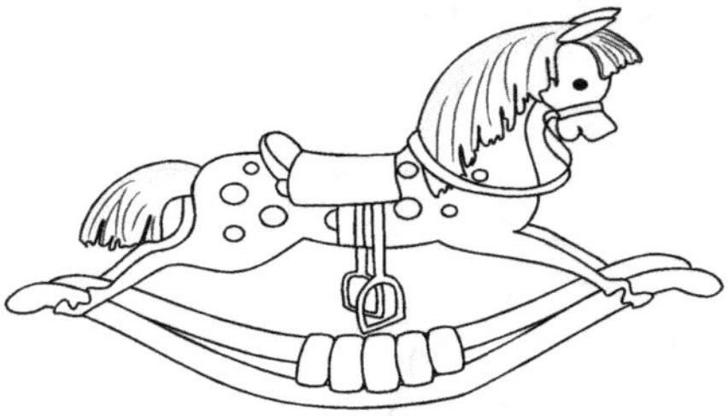

Warm wishes to you!

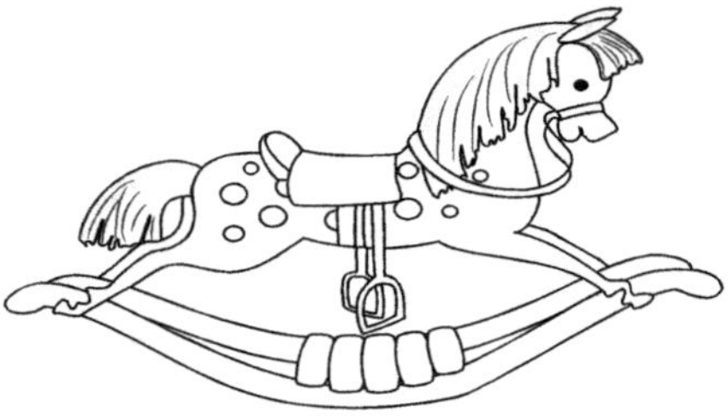

Merry and Bright!

Tis the season to be jolly,
fa la la la la la la la lamb!

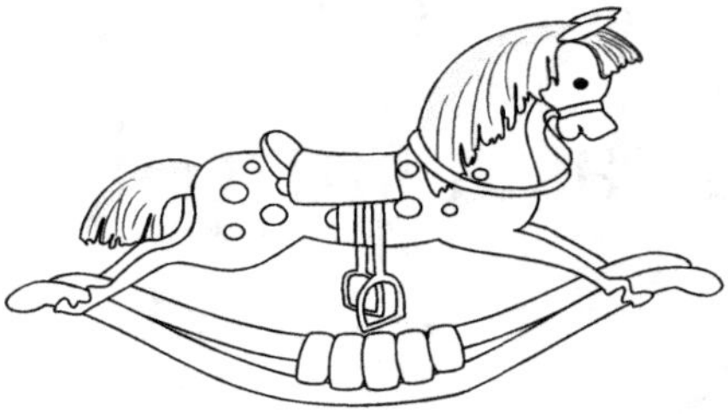

It's the best Christmas ever!

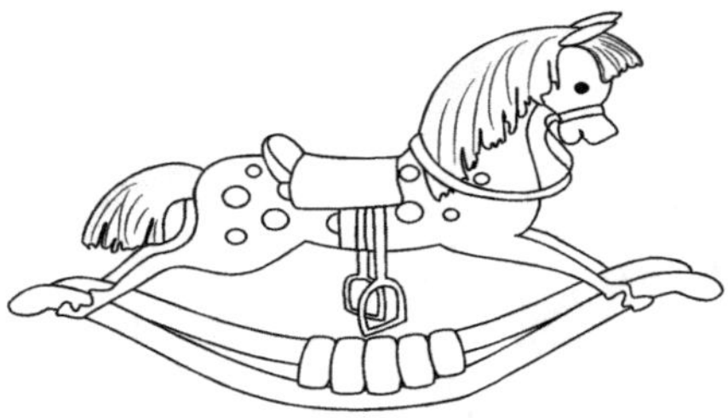

Joy to the animals!

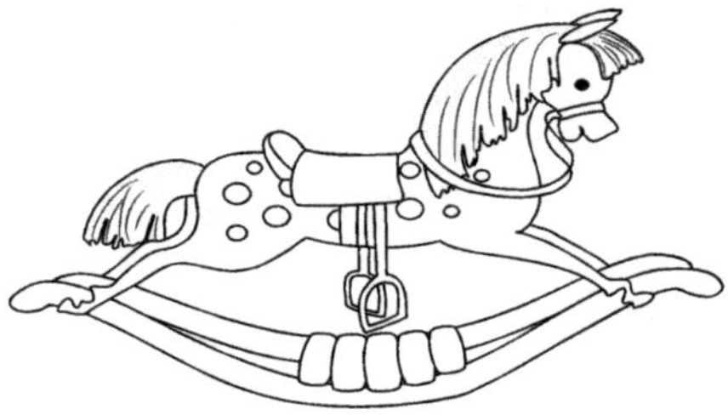

Santa’s magic reindeer!

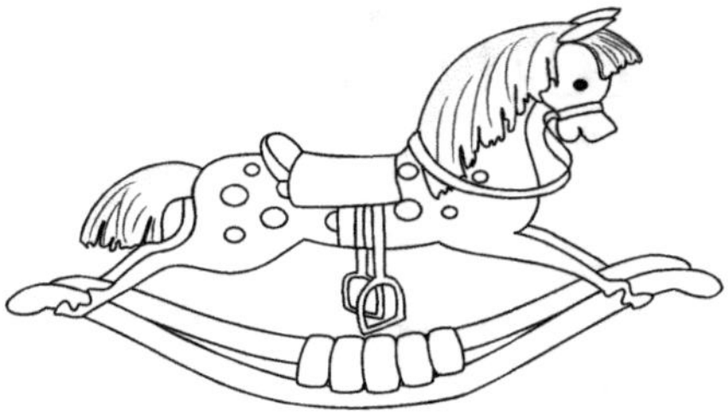

One of Santa’s helpers!

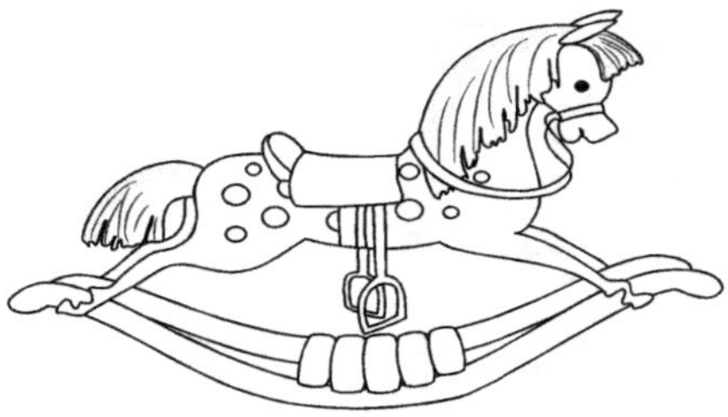

Flying in a winter wonderland!

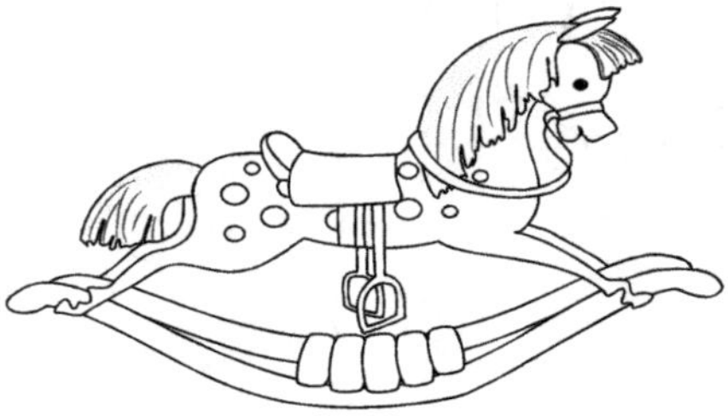

To A Very Sweet Goddaughter!

Merry Christmas

By Florabella Publishing, LLC

www.ingramcontent.com/pod-product-compliance
Lightning Source LLC
Chambersburg PA
CBHW060828260726
48660CB00003B/1147
* 9 7 8 1 9 7 9 7 0 0 8 1 8 *